Super Secret Undercover Campfire Badges

*

(Duct tape campfire badge)

Cool Ideas to make any meeting or campout more livelier enriching and more FUN.

By Greg Cieply

Copyright 2013 Greg Cieply

Super Secret Undercover Campfire Badges

Table of Contents

Intro		5
Chapter 1	Duct Tape Campfire Badge	11
Chapter 2	Video Games Campfire Badge	13
Chapter 3	Connections Campfire Badge	15
Chapter 4	Cards Campfire Badge	17
Chapter 5	Stand-up Comedy/Tall Tales Badge	19
Chapter 6	Detective Campfire Badge	21
Chapter 7	Rock & Roll Campfire Badge	23
Chapter 8	Movies Campfire Badge	25
Chapter 9	Men's Fashion Campfire Badge	27
Chapter 10	Troop Heritage Campfire Badge	31
Chapter 11	Ghost Stories Campfire Badge	33
Chapter 12	Edible Camp Campfire Badge	35
Chapter 13	Fine Dining Campfire Badge	39
Chapter 14	Metal Detecting Campfire Badge	41
Chapter 15	Woodcutting Campfire Badge	43

Chapter 16	Magic Campfire Badge	45
Chapter 17	Riddles Campfire Badge	47
Chapter 18	Science Fair Campfire Badge	49
Appendix A		51
Completion Check List		55

NOTE -

*While this book is written mainly for boys involved in the Scouting program, it will be a great resource for **all boys** who enjoy doing, learning, having fun and who are, at heart, curious about life in general. Parents and leaders who participate will also enjoy the topics and especially the camaraderie they will encounter in the process.*

Most of these are activities that can be done anywhere, but they have been written with group activities in mind.

If you are not a Scout or a Scouting parent, you can substitute "Boy(s)" for the word Scout anytime you come across it

Introduction

Merit badges are a lot of fun. Scouts learn a lot from them as well. It's said that many a Scout gains a lifelong hobby or even his life's vocation from work he did on a merit badge. These are all great things.

But merit badges can also be a lot of work, taking precious time away from family, school and plain old rest. Often I've wished that my son and the Scouts in his troop could simply work on a portion of a merit badge just to sample it and see if they like it.

However since we are in such an achievement culture nowadays, there is almost no parent, Scout leader, fellow Scout or even a sibling who wouldn't try to coerce a Scout to complete a badge he's already started (come on, you can admit it!). It seems the completion of the badge becomes the goal rather than the knowledge or experience that comes with the work. However, to me, the journey is just as important as the destination!

Furthermore if you are like me, you know there are certain subjects that you end up talking to your Scouts about, sometimes in a roundabout way due to the sensitive nature of the topic. Some topics just aren't usually associated with the "outdoor" Scouting program, but are definitely character builders. And sometimes a topic just doesn't seem serious enough to dig any deeper.

And then there's the other side of the time crunch issue. How often at summer camp or on a campout do you notice that the Scouts are really just wasting time doing something not only unproductive, but sometimes downright wrong? (Teasing, hazing, or just general goofing off.) Yeah well, they're probably bored. And since I know that most troops have great leaders and youth who plan their campouts, sometimes they just do things too quickly or cut corners and then they are out of things to do.

So while I'm all for giving them a break and letting them just enjoy taking it easy, I thought that the best way to kill two birds with one stone would be to give them something that leaders and or parents can somewhat justify as being important or even necessary, enlightening, productive and even fun.

We all know that momentum is a great thing. Asking a Scout to try starting one of the major merit badges can be quite daunting. However, asking them to start something easy like one of these campfire badges can lead to greater discovery down the road. Success breeds success!

The "Campfire" badges below are of course NOT OFFICIAL. They fulfill no rank advancements that I am aware of. They will make you think, make you laugh and they will make you scratch your head sometimes. Most importantly, they're a lot of fun. None of them should take more than 30 minutes to complete – some as little as just 5 minutes. And all of them can and should be taught by other parents and even other Scouts.

I'd suggest you run these in a couple of ways. At summer camp, you can have a contest to see who gets the most. In that case, you should have enough parents to offer all of them. Or you could choose to do a couple just for fun on a weekend camp out, or even in conjunction with weekly troop activities at a meeting.

Some of them are harder than others, but none are really comparable to a regular merit badge in terms of effort. Most are highly customizable. Lastly, most of them have a good amount of FUN!

PREPARATION:

Before starting out to camp make sure you assign a leader, older scout or a scout with specific skills to be a "counselor" for each of these badges. Have them read the specific activity they are working on and check the listing at the bottom for any items they might need to bring. To make this successful you should definitely check that they have the items before you leave for camp.

There is a check list at the end of the book that you can use just like the handbook. There are no patches for these yet since they aren't official, but you can always get some stickers or use a stamp that depicts one of the badges (ask a mom who scrapbooks. I'm sure you will find plenty of them in your troop). That always seems to work.

Finally, I know you will have as much fun with these as we have and I hope you enjoy the process and not just the achievements.

Chapter 1: Duct Tape Campfire Badge

"Duct tape is like the Force. It has a light side, a dark side, and it holds the universe together."

– Carl Zwanzig

Duct tape is one of the most versatile items EVER created by man. There is no other tool that can be so helpful to so many people. Developed by a division of Johnson & Johnson in 1942 during World War II, it was made to be a new adhesive tape for the U.S. military, intended to seal ammunition cases against moisture. The tape was required to be ripped by hand, not cut with scissors. This unnamed product was made of thin cotton "duck tape" coated in waterproof polyethylene (plastic) with a layer of rubber-based gray adhesive. It was easy to apply and remove, and was soon adapted to repair military equipment quickly, including vehicles and weapons. This tape, colored in army-standard matte olive drab, was nicknamed "duct tape" by the soldiers.

After completing this badge, it is highly unlikely you will ever NOT be able to consider using duct tape for some purpose. Here's your chance to get the most out of it!

Do two of the following:

A. Make a useful camp gadget using duct tape. (A hat, a wallet, a shirt, an umbrella, the choices are endless!)
B. Repair or improve an item around camp using duct tape.
C. Tape a piece of duct tape to your chest and then rip it off. (OK, this one is only for the bravest (or least hairiest) among you. Try at your own risk!)
2. Arrange a game of Duct Tape pick up. Choose teams with one member who is to be wrapped in tape with the "sticky" side out...then each member, after being carefully lowered to the ground, rolls around trying to pick up as many wads of crumpled paper as possible off of the ground. The first team to collect the most in a preset time – one or two minutes – wins.

Items needed: Roll of duct tape, camera

Chapter 2: Video Game Merit Badge

"It's horrible when you have to watch your child suffer doing homework that is really hard. It's even worse when you spend $50 on a video game and they tell you it's too easy!!"
— Unknown

Depending on when you read this, there may or may not already be a Video Game Merit Badge available from the BSA. However, that doesn't mean you can't learn a little more about games, game development and each other while having some fun around the campfire.

We once spent almost an entire day of backpacking at Philmont Scout Ranch just talking about our favorite games and the conversation swerved into many different directions, including some of the requirements below.

Do three of the following :

A. Learn about one of the first video games available in the home.

B. Tell about your top 3 video games of all time and why you like them.

C. Find out the hardest part in any video game for 3 different leaders or Scouts.

D. Explain what a "Boss" is and name one you have battled.

E. Begin or participate in a campfire round where each person in the circle has to hum or sing a theme song or the background music from ANY video game. Each one has to be different – they can only be used once! If you miss a round, you are out.

Items needed: Scouts and leaders with knowledge of video games (won't be too hard to find!)

Chapter 3: Connections Merit Badge

"We cannot live only for ourselves. A thousand fibers connect us with our fellow men; and among those fibers, as sympathetic threads, our actions run as causes, and they come back to us as effects."
— Herman Melville

One of the best ways to make a summer camp week more enjoyable is to get to know a lot of the people there. If you have ever participated in a group get-together and they started off the meeting with an icebreaker, you'll know what I'm talking about. While you may grimace at first that you have to talk to someone you don't know, for the remainder of the week, you seem to have a new acquaintances everywhere. When you know someone a little more than everyone else, it makes all you have to do together much easier and more enjoyable. Who knows, sometimes you can make a friend for life!

Do two of the following (best done at summer camp):

A. Get the full name of at least 3 counselors – including middle name.

B. Find 3 adult leaders from another troop or staff members who have a birthday that month – GET THEIR FULL NAMES.

C. Take a picture of 3 different counselors posing like they are performing an Olympic event.

D. Find 3 other Scouts who enjoy a hobby that you are passionate about. Tell your counselor about each one.

Items needed: Paper and pen or pencil. Camera

Chapter 4: Cards Campfire Badge

"The game of poker exemplifies the worst aspects of capitalism that have made our country so great."
– Walter Matthau

OK, I know many of you reading this are thinking - "Cards? No poker here! As gambling really has no place in Scouting unless you enjoy the act itself, it really has no redeeming qualities whatsoever. But cards in general are not only about gambling. They are a just as wholesome as Scrabble, Monopoly and Dominos if played correctly. Playing any kind of card game is a great way to kill time, promote fellowship and even learn strategy and tactics. However, if your Scout doesn't know even the basic premise of most games other than Go Fish, it will no doubt make for some awkward moments in his high school and college days. Why not learn some strategies and maybe even have some fun? Some of these games will take an adult to teach them and some will take the mentality of a young boy to play! You can bet that you'll smile when they all gather around to play Cribbage on the train to Philmont - because you taught them the game!

Do three of the following:

A. Learn the basic rules of Gin Rummy.

B. Learn the basics of either cribbage, euchre or Hearts. Tell your counselor about them.

C. Successfully start any kind of game with at least 4 Scouts and teach them all to play.

D. Play a game of War or Slapjack with one of your leaders.

E. Learn a card trick from your counselor

Items needed: Deck of cards, rule book/instructions for card games, several card tricks – you'll need more than just one!

Chapter 5: Stand-Up Comedy/Tall Tales Campfire Badge

"Why ruin a good story with the truth?"
– Woody Allen

Scouting is about camping, and what is camping without a "campfire"? If you've ever been camping, you'll know that the more memorable campfires were the ones that had some kind of entertainment – stories, songs, skits, etc. While many Scouts participate in skits and even songs, it's not often they are asked to get up and tell a story all alone, much less try to make a whole group of people laugh. This is the opportunity to do so in a safe and pleasant environment among good friends. Just being able to get up and talk in front of others is a great confidence builder and should be part of all merit badges. It's even better when you get to make them laugh!

Do one of the following:

A. With the help of your counselor write and perform a 1-minute stand-up comedy routine where you tell jokes or do an impersonation based on something or someone at camp. Keep it clean!

B. Tell a tall tale – phony story – at a campfire. Your tale must last at least 1 minute and be based on something or someone you have seen at camp.

C. Write your own skit based on a recent event you encountered at camp or a TV show or commercial that is popular at the moment. This should be a parody of the actual event or show. This should last at least 1 minute.

D. Sing a funny campfire song and get an adult to join in!

Items needed: Good attitude, good voice, sense of humor!

Chapter 6: Detective Campfire Badge

"Very few of us are what we seem"
– Agatha Christie

Solving mysteries can be a lot of fun. Everyone remembers the game CLUE. Many people have participated in Murder Mystery parties. It's fun to find and interpret clues along with the camaraderie of other friends joining in.

Do 2 of the following:

A. Solve a camp mystery story – successfully choose the "killer." One person acts as the host. The host does not play but must select a murderer and a detective. He does this duck-duck-goose style, by asking everyone in the group to sit in a circle with eyes closed. He then selects a murderer by tapping on someone's head twice and a detective by tapping on someone else's head once. When all eyes are open, the detective sits in the middle, and the murderer must begin "killing" fellow campers by winking at them. The objective for the murderer is to do his killing without getting caught. The detective is charged with figuring out who is doing all this winking. The idea for everyone else is to die, when they are winked at, in dramatic and glorious fashion. Throughout the course of game play, the detective makes three guesses as to who the murderer is. If he guesses correctly, he becomes the host. If he doesn't nab the killer, he must remain the detective for another round of murder.

B. Put on a game of "Thief" at camp: Choose an object larger than the size of a basketball. Choose a location it needs to be taken to and a prize for getting it there. Secretly choose one person in the camp and tell them that he is the "Thief" and that he has to get the object to that place before getting caught. Let him know that no one else will know he is the thief beforehand. Then tell all the other campers – without letting the other campers know – that there is a thief in camp who will try to get that object to the location and they need to stop him. If the thief gets there first with the object, they win!

C. Two Truths and a Lie – campfire is a perfect time to tell stories about the past and converse with friends. In Two Truths and a Lie, players take turns telling the other players two surprising truths about their past experiences and then add one lie about an experience they never actually had. The other players must guess which of the three experiences is a lie.

Items needed: Good attitude, good voice, inquisitive mind – no cape or pipe needed!

Chapter 7: Rock & Roll Campfire Badge

"Rock & roll is here to stay"
– Neil Young

Rock & roll would probably fit under the Music Merit Badge offered by the BSA, but it's not generally something you would focus on exclusively. Considering how impactful this art form has been on the culture, spawning so many other forms of music, it would be helpful for anyone to know how it came about. It might even open up some doors to a career, if not just a new interest. At a minimum, doing this with an adult would help the Scouts to get to know them better.

Do 2 of the following:

A. Find out about 3 distinct types of rock & roll

B. Name 5 famous rock & roll bands and learn one of their greatest hits from your counselor.

C. Ask 3 adults their favorite rock & roll bands and why they like them.

D. Find out what is considered the first rock & roll song.

E. Play a rock & roll song, or at least a few lines of one, at a campfire using any instrument.

Items needed: Anyone who knows and enjoys rock & roll!

Chapter 8: Movies Campfire Badge

"Never judge a book by its movie"
– J.W. Eagan

The first machine patented in the United States that showed animated pictures or movies was a device called the "wheel of life" or "zoopraxiscope." Patented in 1867 by William Lincoln, moving drawings or photographs were watched through a slit in the zoopraxiscope. This crude form of showing action somewhere other than in real life would not gain much popularity until 1891 and the invention by the Edison company of the Kinetoscope, which enabled one person at a time to view moving pictures. This was not an easy process until the first motion picture camera was created by the Frenchman Louis Lumiere in 1896. Ever since then we have had the ability to finally see how a picture was worth 1000 words.

Everyone has their favorite movie and this is usually for all kinds of reasons – content, visuals, special effects, actors, etc. Find out more about this and make some bonds with your fellow Scouts or leaders:

Do two of the following:

A. At a campfire, tell your troop about your favorite movie and why it is a favorite.

B. Get a collection of 10 movies that all Scouts in your troop must see from any of your troop leaders or camp leaders. Tell your counselor about them.

C. Name two of the most famous actors and actresses who were famous for movies they did before your year of birth.

Chapter 9: Men's Fashion Campfire Badge

"Every generation laughs at the old fashions, but follows religiously the new."
– Henry David Thoreau

What is this doing in a book for Scouts about camping, you might ask? Well, after learning to tie a bow tie by watching it online, I realized that not only was I ignorant about that, but also about lots of other things when it came to fashion and especially men's fashion. Now we are certainly not, as a gender, as attentive to our outward appearance as the fairer sex, but there is a need to look good at times. At a minimum, all boys should have an idea of what the standards are for men's attire. Whether this be for a job interview, a business meeting, a formal event or even a date, let's face it, first impressions count. And if we want our Scouts to succeed, we should not simply leave this up to chance or circumstances. We can give them a quick taste of what to look for and how to present themselves, and maybe even learn a few things for ourselves as parents and leaders. This one will require that you bring a few things on a camp out. You may want to consider doing this one at a regular troop meeting.

I can guarantee that at some point every boy will need to know how to tie a tie. At a minimum, here's your chance to make sure they are familiar with it.

    A. Learn to tie a regular tie knot.

Do 3 of the following:

B. Learn to tie a Windsor knot.

C. Learn to tie a bow tie.

D. Learn to fold a pocket square and tell where it goes.

E. Tell your counselor the difference between a sport jacket, a 3-piece, a 2-piece and a double-breasted suit.

F. Successfully put on a pair of cuff links.

G. Successfully put on a pair of suspenders.

H. Explain what a tuxedo is and where and when you would wear one.

I. Ask your counselor or other leaders what different kinds of formal men's shoes are worn and when you should wear them.

Chapter 10: Troop Heritage Campfire Badge

"History is the version of past events that people have decided to agree upon."
– Napoleon Bonaparte

Knowing where you came from is an important part of life. However, it's not always possible to know all the details. As anyone involved in Scouting will know, there is a Scouting Heritage Merit Badge, and for anyone who wants to know more about the Scouting program, I would highly recommend working on it. However, sitting around the campfire, with a bunch of your fellow troop members, you should have no problem working on this one.

Do 3 of the following:

A. Find out how old your troop is and who founded it.

B. Name the last 3 Scoutmasters.

C. Name the last 5 Senior Patrol Leaders.

D. Name the last 3 Eagle Scouts or 5 in any order.

E. Find the names of some the summer camps your troop has attended in the past.

F. Find out the last high adventure trip your troop did and who attended.

\ \

Chapter 11: Ghost Stories Campfire Badge

"It's easier to dismiss ghosts in the daylight."

— Patricia Briggs

Who doesn't love the suspense of being out in the dark, sitting in front of a roaring fire and hearing a story about something coming from out of the woods? There is probably no better place to hear, much less tell, a good ghost story. Most good ghost stories involve someone, something or some area that everyone listening can directly relate to. It really helps if you can personalize the story to your own troop. So making up one of your own is the best way to do it.

Caution: if you plan on enlisting a leader to help you "scare" some of the Scouts, don't be surprised if you get more of a reaction than you were looking for. A scary story in a dark outdoor setting can sometimes be too real for some Scouts and even leaders. While ghost stories always seem to be part of camping in general, there is always the chance of something going awry. Know your audience and know your story.

Doing a ghost tour can be a lot of fun but it will require the efforts of a leader or two. Sometimes a camp will have a lore of hauntings that the camp directors are aware of. Ask around if you can. Otherwise, make up your own! There are plenty of stories you can adapt to your own situation.

Do 2 of the following:

A. Learn what makes a good ghost story from your counselor.

B. Ask 3 leaders if they can tell you about a favorite or memorable ghost story they can recall.

C. Tell a ghost story at a campfire – either one you have created or one you learn from a book or a leader.

D. Help create a ghost tour of your camp.

Chapter 12: Edible Camp Campfire Badge

"Edible, adj.: Good to eat and wholesome to digest, as a worm to a toad, as a toad to a snake, as a snake to a pig, a pig to a man, and a man to a worm"

— Ambrose Bierce

So much of Scouting involves the outdoors – camping, hiking, fishing and especially cooking. But when we camp, we lug all our food in and rarely do we live off the land around us. In most environments, there isn't a whole lot you can eat, but I suspect that we don't even look very often. But at certain times and under certain conditions, there is always SOMETHING you can eat – think about those crazy bizarre foods shows on TV. While I'm not suggesting that you ask your Scouts to eat something that might make them sick, there is almost always some kind of berry or fruit or even some kind of tuber available to eat at camp. Most people have no idea. We found out that the common weed "plantain" has a stalk that, when dried, can yield wheat-like kernels that can be ground into flour. Not the best-tasting, but enough to survive on. And then there is the gourmet meal I once ate at the top restaurant in Chicago. Course number 4 was "stinging nettles" soup. It was absolutely delicious. I wouldn't recommend trying this without a little research first, but there is a simple way to prepare it, one that most boys could easily accomplish.

Essentially, if you were stuck on a ship at sea with no food or water, how would you survive, what would you eat or drink? Your campsite is your ship. How would you survive?

Hey, if you give these a try, you might one day shock your friends and family with one of the best meals they have ever had!

A. With the assistance of a counselor or adult leader, find at least 3 different types of plants – including berries, fruit or roots – that can be eaten around your camp or campsite.

B. Cook or make a snack with the help of your counselor using these foods – do not try this alone. Make sure your counselor approves these items. NO MUSHROOMS!

C. Find a flower you can eat – you don't have to consume it – just find any edible ones and confirm they are indeed edible.

Items needed: A strong stomach and willingness to try new things

Chapter 13: Fine Dining Campfire Badge

"Tell me what you eat, and I will tell you what you are."

— Anthelme Brillat Savarin

This is one of those activities that just do not fit in with the Scouting program. However, since we are trying to build character in our young men, it could definitely be useful for them to know about some of the "finer" things in life. This is also one of those items that would likely not be covered by most merit badges and maybe only ever "discussed" by parents or leaders around a campfire.

I don't think there will be much field work on this one at any summer camp, but most adults can offer something along these lines to help a Scout be a little more "refined" when it comes to eating out. At a minimum it could mean learning some table manners – "Scouts actually can do that," you might ask?

Do three of the following:

A. Find out why there is sometimes more than a single fork, knife or spoon at a dinner setting. Find out how to use them properly. Hint – from the outside in!

B. Find out about meal courses and what goes between and after.

C. Find out where to place your napkin. In your lap? As a bib?

D. Give an example of something that would be considered gourmet food.

E. Find out the definition of a "sommelier." Find out about three different types of product he would offer.

F. Find out about three different steak cuts.

G. Find out what "high tea" service is.

H. Ask an adult leader about his or her favorite fine dining experience and what he or she liked about it.

Items needed: A willingness to try new things

Chapter 14: Metal Detecting Campfire Badge

"One of the advantages of being disorderly is that one is constantly making exciting discoveries."
– A.A. Milne

Since "leave no trace" is part of the Scouting program, it seems a bit contradictory to be digging up your campsite. However, when you are making an impact on your surroundings, as you will inevitably do with tents and other items, the small amount of digging with a metal detector will hardly cause much additional impact. Considering the time, effort and fun Scouts will receive from this activity, as well as the neat things they will find, it's definitely worth the tradeoff. If you really have an issue with it, you can leave this one out.

You will need any kind of metal detector for this one. If you can't get one from one of your Scout parents or other friends, I would look on eBay, Craigslist or even at local garage sales. There's no need for anything fancy. I'd caution, though, that this can be addicting and the boys will often fight over who gets to detect and even who gets to dig!

Often the best way to ensure success when digging is to research an area to see if there were any houses or other structures in the area you plan on digging in.

Do the following:

    A. Lean how to use a metal detector from your counselor.

    B. Learn the rules and proper digging etiquette for using your detector from your counselor.

    C. Find at least 3 targets and replace the holes you have dug.

    D. Find out if there are any areas where there used to be a building or some kind of structure near your campsite. See whether you can search that area.

Chapter 15: Woodcutting Badge

"People love chopping wood. In this activity one immediately sees results."
— Albert Einstein

Einstein's words never rang truer than when you are out camping, especially if you are on a longer-term trek of more than a weekend. Often you have no idea what you are going to be doing and what your next steps might be. But when you are chopping wood, there is no illusion as to what you are doing it for and what comes next.

While most Scouts learn how to handle a knife or saw, they usually don't get to "chop" logs. This is a great opportunity to show them the correct techniques as well as get some firewood for the fire. Make sure you have some knowledgeable adult leaders or older Scouts there to supervise. This is not an activity for all. Totin' Chip is definitely required for this one and if you really want to make sure you have enough wood for your week, make this one mandatory – at least they start something!!

Do the following:

A. Learn the best techniques for cutting wood to use for a bonfire.

B. Learn what kind of wood you can and should use.

C. Tell the best way to store the wood you have chopped.

D. Chop/saw all the wood needed for the night's campfire.

Chapter 16: Magic Campfire Badge

"It's still magic even if you know how it's done."
— Terry Pratchett

It would be just as easy to include this as part of the Stand-Up Comedy, Tall Tales Badge, but honestly, performing magic is not for everyone. It takes some inspiration, a bit of practice and even some luck to do even the simplest of tricks. But if you can do it, the rewards are priceless – your friends will be amazed and mystified, and they will all look at you in a different way. If you are up to the task at hand, this could be a lifelong hobby and maybe even a vocation at some point. You won't likely become the next Harry Potter and set off to Hogwarts anytime soon, but you might make the campfire more interesting than anyone would have ever thought.

NOTE: You will need to have a leader who has some background in magic or at least prepares for the camp with some research about magic as well as some items that would allow participants to do some tricks. There are some moderately priced kits that usually have anywhere from 1-100 easy to learn tricks that can be very useful and often are small enough to bring on a camp out.

Do 2 of the following:

A. Learn about the origin of magic from your counselor.

B. Name 2 famous magicians.

C. Tell about 2 tricks you have seen before and how you think the tricks were done.

D. Explain what "sleight of hand" means.

E. Do 3 magic tricks for your counselor or 1 in front of the entire campfire.

Chapter 17: Riddles Campfire Badge

"The riddles of God are more satisfying than the solutions of man."
— Unknown

Riddles have confounded everyone ever born. The challenge of solving them is especially powerful for young boys sitting around a campfire or more appropriately walking or hiking together in a group – ANY group activity works well. The role of the riddle is not just to puzzle people's minds or to make the asker seem smarter than everyone else – although those things will happen. It can also be a way to create some fellowship, get everyone's minds off a difficult task and even simply cure boredom. I can remember many a hike that was certainly shortened due to a few riddles!

This one is quite simple for any Scout to do and will likely pay off in spades over the years.

Do the following:

A. Learn a riddle from 3 Scouts or leaders.

B. Tell a riddle to someone and wait to see if they can guess it.

C. While hiking or sitting at a campfire, ask one of the riddles you learned to the whole troop.

Chapter 18: Science Fair Campfire Badge

"I am often amazed at how much more capability and enthusiasm for science there is among elementary school youngsters than there is among college students."

— Carl Sagan

This is a fun one that the entire camp can do. It's also a real easy way start them out with awards in this book.

Science is indeed more interesting to younger children – at least they express that interest more vocally than older children and adults.

This is another great opportunity to hold an event at camp that will grow some fellowship. It is quick, easy, fun and most of all will kill boredom.

Do 1 of the following:

A. Participate in a campsite/troop egg drop. Find a way to keep your egg from cracking after falling from a height your leaders have chosen (usually 10 feet or more). You may only use natural items sourced from around the camp as your holding device.

B. Be the camp weatherman for a day. Check the forecast with a leader or camp staff. Post it on a camp bulletin board or announce it after breakfast. Include temperature, wind (Beaufort scale) and precipitation forecast.

C. Build a simple "Rube Goldberg" contraption that moves, fills or completes some kind of task using at least 3 different processes.

Do both of the following

D. Calculate the temperature using the "Cricket Scale" – see appendix.

E. Do a leaf test with your counselor. Using at least 5 different leaves or grass – not poison ivy please!! – crush them up or roll them in your hands and smell each one. Remember the smell. Then have someone crush or roll up the same ones and identify them while blindfolded.

Appendix A
Beaufort Scale

Force	Wind (Knots)	WMO Classification	Appearance of Wind Effects On the Water	On Land
0	Less than 1	Calm	Sea surface smooth and mirror-like	Calm, smoke rises vertically
1	1-3	Light Air	Scaly ripples, no foam crests	Smoke drift indicates wind direction, still wind vanes
2	4-6	Light Breeze	Small wavelets, crests glassy, no breaking	Wind felt on face, leaves rustle, vanes begin to move
3	7-10	Gentle Breeze	Large wavelets, crests begin to break, scattered whitecaps	Leaves and small twigs constantly moving, light flags extended
4	11-16	Moderate Breeze	Small waves 1-4 ft becoming longer, numerous whitecaps	Dust, leaves and loose paper lifted, small tree branches move
5	17-21	Fresh Breeze	Moderate	Small trees

			waves 4-8 ft taking longer form, many whitecaps, some spray	in leaf begin to sway
6	22-27	Strong Breeze	Larger waves 8-13 ft, whitecaps common, more spray	Larger tree branches moving, whistling in wires
7	28-33	Near Gale	Sea heaps up, waves 13-19 ft, white foam streaks off breakers	Whole trees moving, resistance felt walking against wind
8	34-40	Gale	Moderately high (18-25 ft) waves of greater length, edges of crests begin to break into spindrift, foam blown in streaks	Twigs breaking off trees, generally impedes progress
9	41-47	Strong Gale	High waves (23-32 ft), sea begins to roll, dense streaks of foam, spray may reduce visibility	Slight structural damage occurs, slate blows off roofs
10	48-55	Storm	Very high waves (29-41	Seldom experienced

52

			ft) with overhanging crests, sea white with densely blown foam, heavy rolling, lowered visibility	on land, trees broken or uprooted, "considerable structural damage"
11	56-63	Violent Storm	Exceptionally high (37-52 ft) waves, foam patches cover sea, visibility more reduced	
12	64+	Hurricane	Air filled with foam, waves over 45 ft, sea completely white with driving spray, visibility greatly reduced	

Cricket Scale

Step 1: Go outside in the evening to a place where you can hear crickets. Try to listen for the chirp of just one cricket.

Step 2: Count its chirps for 14 seconds.

Step 3: Write down the number, and then add 40 to it.

The sum will tell you the temperature in degrees Fahrenheit -- those are cricket degrees!

Campfire Merit Badge Completion List

Duct Tape Campfire Badge

Completed _____

Counselor_____

Video Games Campfire Badge

Completed _____

Counselor_____

Connections Campfire Badge

Completed _____

Counselor_____

Cards Campfire Badge

Completed _____

Counselor_____

Stand-up Comedy/Tall Tales Badge

Completed _____

Counselor_____

Detective Campfire Badge

Completed _____

Counselor_____

Rock & Roll Campfire Badge

Completed _____

Counselor_____

Movies Campfire Badge

Completed _____

Counselor_____

Men's Fashion Campfire Badge

Completed _____

Counselor_____

Troop Heritage Campfire Badge

Completed _____

Counselor_____

Ghost Stories Campfire Badge

Completed _____

Counselor _____

Edible Camp Campfire Badge

Completed _____

Counselor _____

Fine Dining Campfire Badge

Completed _____

Counselor _____

Metal Detecting Campfire Badge

Completed _____

Counselor_____

Woodcutting Campfire Badge

Completed _____

Counselor_____

Magic Campfire Badge

Completed _____

Counselor_____

Riddles Campfire Badge

Completed _____

Counselor_____

Science Fair Campfire Badge

Completed _____

Counselor_____

Made in the USA
Columbia, SC
08 January 2021